THE MASTER KEY

THE MASTER KEY

THE MASTER KEY TO COMPLETE FINANCIAL FREEDOM

STACEY M. OLIVER

South Carolina

Printed and Published in the United States of
America

The Master Key: The Master Key to Complete
Financial Freedom/ STACEY M. OLIVER

ISBN-13: 978-1530953394

Interior Designs by STACEY M. OLIVER

ACKNOWLEDGEMENTS

I would like to thank God for all things and for the wisdom and creative ideas. To our sons, Uriah and Benaiah, thank you for your motivation and encouragement. Thank you to all my family and friends who I hold dear to my heart.

CONTENTS

INTRODUCTION

We've all been there ...
You've spent more money than you had. You've counted the money before receiving it. You started making more money just to create more debt.   You spent the bonus money instead of investing it.   You continue living from paycheck to paycheck.   You've racked your brain and stressed yourself out, trying to come up with the very best budget, which you found yourself having to tweak every month. You've started this journey called the snowball effect, but when you looked at your finances, you still ended up robbing Peter to pay Paul.

Why?   You noticed you didn't include funds in the budget for an emergency, for a dream vacation, for a charitable donation, and most of all, funds to pay yourself.

Does it feel like your financial freedom is locked away, far from your reach?

Complete financial freedom can be a challenge when you don't have the key to success to secure your finances. But I have great news for you today... It's time to throw away all the other keys you have been using to unlock doors to your financial success.

Get ready to become empowered with the Master Key to complete financial freedom.

1, 2, 3 Here We Go!

I

BARRIERS

Do you know what is keeping the doors locked to you accessing total financial freedom? What is the thing standing in your way, keeping you from obtaining financial success? The answer to both questions is simple, Barrier(s).

Barriers prohibit access to complete financial freedom.

A barrier is an obstacle that prevents movement, prevents access, and it will even prevent progress. In other words, a barrier will frustrate, hinder, limit, and restrict your financial approach to gaining access to complete financial success!

The trend of financial barriers (obstacles) can filter and recycle through you and/or your family.

Barriers will frustrate, hinder, limit, and restrict your financial wealth.

- What is your barrier? Or should I ask, what is your major barrier (the root cause of why you are in the state you're in)?

- What is hindering your progress to gaining complete financial freedom? Is it your nonresistance to over spending?

- What door is your total financial freedom locked behind? Is it the door of dishonesty? It may be the door of procrastination. Or is it the door of indifference?

- Is your mindset serving as a barrier against your absolute economic power?

You could be the obstacle blockading your entrance to the world of financial freedom. Rate yourself (page 18) to see if you are indeed the obstacle.

Rate Yourself
(1 = somewhat, 2 = rarely, 3 = almost always,
4 = always)

Determined   1 2 3 4
(-firm decision; adamant; unwavering)

Self-motivated   1 2 3 4
(-without supervision; initiative to undertake)

Self-discipline   1 2 3 4
(-overcome one's weaknesses; the ability to make
yourself do things that should be done)

Self-control   1 2 3 4
(-the ability to manage your actions, feelings, and
emotions)

Persistent   1 2 3 4
(-continuing firmly in a course of action despite
difficulty/opposition; continuing to endure over a
prolonged period; preserving; lasting; enduring)

Determination, self-motivation, self-discipline, self-control, and persistence are necessary qualities to being financially stabled and to live a life of abundance.

A locked door must be unlocked to gain access to what is inside. Before you can gain access to the door you must possess the key to unlocking the door. Before you can possess the key to unlocking the door, you must identify the barrier that stands in the way of you getting to the door to unlock it.

Identify and list your barrier(s). _____

_____

_____

_____

_____

_____

_____

_____

_____

_____

_____

_____

_____

_____

_____

Comments_____

_____

_____

_____

_____

_____

_____

_____

_____

_____

II

TYPES OF BARRIERS

Barriers that confine you to your past:

1. If I haven't grown up having little, then I wouldn't be over my head in debt;

2. I didn't have anyone to show or teach me how to be a good money manager;

3. I didn't have the knowledge or the how to make my money work for me instead of me working so hard for my money;

4. I didn't have the same opportunity others had;

Are you confined to your past by one of these barriers? If so, which one?

_____

_____

_____

_____

_____

_____

_____

_____

_____

_____

_____

_____

_____

_____

_____

_____

_____

_____

_____

_____

_____

_____

_____

Barriers that limit your movement to progress:

1. I never made enough money to save or invest;

2. I never thought about my creditworthiness;

3. I don't know how to make my dreams a reality;

4. I don't believe I can be completely financially free;

Is a barrier limiting your progress? If so, what barrier?

_____

_____

_____

_____

_____

_____

_____

_____

_____

_____

Barriers that barricade our positive thinking:

1. I've heard about financial security, but I haven't done anything to obtain it;

2. I never thought about the cost of funeral or burial expenses;

3. I'm not good at planning ahead;

4. I'll start saving later not now;

What barrier is barricading your positive thinking?

_____
_____
_____
_____
_____
_____
_____
_____
_____
_____
_____

III

BARRIERS BECOME BURDENS

Financial barriers become financial burdens. Just think about it and ask yourself these three questions.

1. Am I financially prepared, without any doubt, to take care of any type of emergency?

   _____

2. Do I have an exit plan such as Retirement, Employee to Business Owner, Preneed Care, or a Legacy?

   _____

3. Am I able to make more than $1,000 charitable cash contribution or investment on the spot without hesitation? _____

Did you answer "No" to any of the above questions? If so, you just discovered a financial barrier that will soon become a financial burden for you and/or your family if you do not act and start making preparation now.

Don't allow your barriers to become burdens.

Action Plan

_____

_____

_____

_____

_____

_____

_____

_____

_____

_____

_____

_____

_____

_____

_____

_____

_____

_____

_____

_____

IV

BARRIERS COMPARABLE TO BURDENS

Financial barriers are much the same as viruses. Financial viruses of this world are killing families...Yes! Financial viruses such as,

- uncontrollable spending

- non-budgeting

- no financial stability

- over-indebtedness

- lack of integrity

If individuals are not trained, taught, and/or lead by examples, financial viruses continue to move from one family to the next due to the lack of knowledge of financial literacy. From my experience, stomach viruses will run rapidly through your entire household until everyone has contracted the virus unless someone takes the initiative to proactively kill the germ of the virus. The financial barrier germ must be destroyed. If the financial barrier is not broken and destroyed in our lives, there will not be a financial legacy left for our next generation.

The germ agent of financial barriers is highly contagious; therefore, it must be obliterated.

Will you take the charge to demolish the financial barrier in your family lineage? Be affirmative! You make the change. You start speaking the language of financial freedom. Tell yourself, "I will no longer allow unnecessary debt to dictate my financial status".

Action Plan

_____

_____

_____

_____

_____

_____

_____

_____

_____

_____

_____

_____

_____

_____

_____

_____

_____

_____

_____

_____

_____

V

ELIMINATING BARRIERS

All barriers have one main purpose. They allow you to not or never achieve financial freedom. Negative thinking prevents us from gaining access to the doors to our entire financial freedom. Whatsoever we think concerning our finances, so are we.

For as he thinketh in his heart, so is he:
Proverbs 23:7 (KJV)

From what I think, I will speak. If I think I'm broke, I will say I'm broke. If I think I will never have anything, then I will find myself speaking it. To secure our financial freedom with the key of success, we must *first* rid ourselves of the negatives.

Negative words are first a thought before they are ever spoken.

Stop allowing the doors to remain locked to your financial freedom. Start changing your financial status today! A financial assessment (page 34) is a great way to pinpoint your present financial standing.

Complete the financial assessment to
determine your financial status.

(Set a timeline (page. 37) for the item(s) you need to do or change.)

1. Do you know your net worth?

_____

(Net worth is what is owned minus
what is owed.)

2. Do you have a nest egg?

_____

(Nest egg is another word for
retirement savings.)

3. Do you have a legal will?

_____

4. Have you reviewed your credit report lately? If so, when?

_____

(If you have not received or reviewed your credit report within the past year, request a copy of your report today.)

5. Are you living from paycheck to paycheck?

_____

Now that you have assessed your financial status, you are ready to take the step to possessing the key to complete financial freedom.

Comments_____

_____

_____

_____

_____

_____

_____

_____

_____

_____

_____

Timeline Notes

_____

_____

_____

_____

_____

_____

_____

_____

_____

_____

_____

_____

_____

_____

_____

_____

_____

_____

_____

_____

VI

RID YOURSELF OF THE NEGATIVES

It is time to destroy financial barriers instead of the barriers destroying us by keeping us as hostages in captivity. I challenge you to stop with the negative thinking which produces negative words and start with positive, creative thinking which produces positive, powerful words.

Positive, creative thinking produces positive, powerful words.

Stop and Start Exercise

- Stop thinking and saying I can't - Start saying I can.
- Stop improvising - Start planning.
- Stop being unproductive - Start being productive.
- Stop just dreaming - Start living the dream.
- Stop doubting - Start believing.
- Stop spending - Start saving.
- Stop saying I don't have - Start saying I do have.
- Stop neglecting change - Start being the change.
- Stop saying it won't work - Start saying it will work.
- Stop saying I'm broke - Start saying I'm wealthy.

Declare what you will STOP and START.

Choose and write a phrase from the start and stop exercise (page 39).

_____

_____

_____

_____

_____

_____

_____

_____

_____

_____

_____

_____

_____

_____

_____

_____

_____

_____

_____

_____

_____

_____

Every day, begin reading aloud the saying you chose. As you begin practicing it, you will notice your speech changing as your thinking process is being trained to think differently regarding your finances and financial state. For example; **Stop saying I'm broke, and <u>Start</u> saying I'm wealthy**. As you read it and say it aloud every day, it will become second nature for you to think and speak wealth.

You have begun to blockade (remove or eliminate) the barriers that kept you from approaching and unlocking the doors of your financial freedom.

Comments_____

_____

_____

_____

_____

_____

_____

_____

_____

_____

VII

CUSTOMIZED MASTER KEY

Each one of our barriers is different from the other. Even if they are the same, they are different in some way because we are uniquely and wonderfully made. That's why WE need to be empowered with OUR own customized "Master Key".

Empowered with a customized "Master Key"

Why do I need the "Master Key" and not just a key? A "Master Key" allows you to open several locks which also have their own key. To ensure all my financial doors are unlocked, I only need the "Master Key" to unlock the doors to my positive thinking, to being financially wealthy, to becoming a well-balanced money manager, to my financial security and to my total financial freedom.

Access has been granted to you today to possessing the "Master Key" to eradicating the negativity you have in your mind and affirm it with a yes.

Eradicate the negativity in your mind and affirm it with a yes!

Now that access has been granted, you can begin to destroy the negative thinking and affirm it with positive thinking. To change your old way of thinking, you must think the opposite of the way you were accustomed to thinking. The past thoughts of "I can't", "It won't work" and "It's not enough", can be destroyed with the thoughts of "I can", "It will work" and "It's more than enough".

Developing a new way of thinking is simple. Look at it this way: think the opposite of the way you use to think. If you were accustomed to thinking offensively when it came to money, then begin to think defensively. One thing for sure, everything wanted is not needed to sustain sound financial well-being.

Wants are not a priority when it comes to sustaining sound financial well-being.

There is a cliché, "You tell one lie, you must tell another to cover the first lie". Well, the same with our thought process. You start thinking positively, you will continue to think positively more often. But you must train yourself.   It does not happen automatically.

If you are serious about transitioning your current financial condition to one of higher prestige, recite the Financial Declaration on page 47 – 48 daily to ensure your accountability to changing the trend of financial barriers (obstacles) from filtering and recycling through you and/or your family.

FINANCIAL DECLARATION

I have been empowered to possess the *"Master Key"* to take charge of my financial wealth, so I can begin to experience financial freedom; I must do my part. I hereby commit to changing the attitude and lifestyle that keep me in financial bondage, and I dedicate myself to becoming an effective, disciplined money manager over what I already have and all things to come.

I declare I have a positive mindset, and I am determined, self-motivated, and persistent to obtaining the key to maintaining complete financial freedom. I will break the financial barriers starting now!

Then I, _____,
will give...

  Without fear
  With pleasure
  Liberally...

Because I, _____,

am confident, and I now hold the *"Master Key"* to my financial FREE-DOM.

Date_____

I present to you your **Master Key**! Continue to possess the *KEY* to unlock the doors to your Financial *FREEDOM.*

1, 2, 3 Let's Go!

Remember to stop negative thinking. Start eliminating the barriers, now that access has been granted. You now possess your own customized Master Key.

ACTIVITIES

Perhaps you are a Bible reader; here are some wealth scripts below pertaining to financial freedom. There are many more scriptures in the Bible about wealth. Start with these, one at a time, and add to them as you continue to transform your mindset and speech toward your finances.

Wealth Scripts

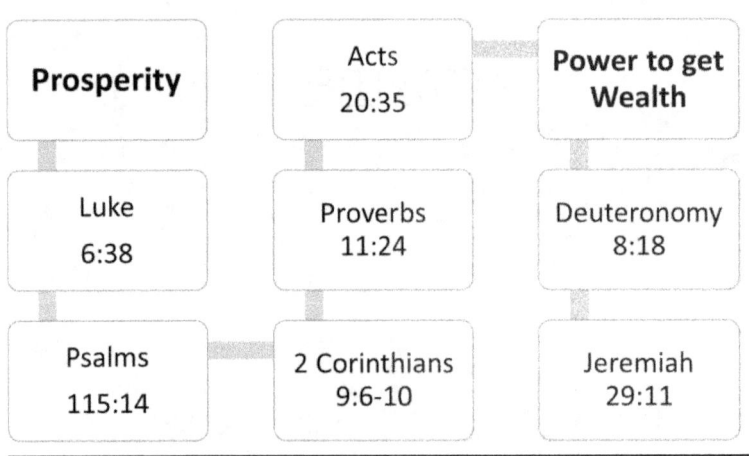

Prosperity	Acts 20:35	**Power to get Wealth**
Luke 6:38	Proverbs 11:24	Deuteronomy 8:18
Psalms 115:14	2 Corinthians 9:6-10	Jeremiah 29:11

Challenge: As you add to the wealth scripts, group them appropriately as shown above.

Comments_____

_____

_____

_____

_____

_____

_____

_____

_____

_____

_____

Test your knowledge by matching the verse to each scripture below.

Match Scripts

Luke 6:38	• But thou shalt remember the LORD thy God: for it is He that giveth thee power to get wealth.....
Psalm 115:14	• The LORD shall increase you more and more, you and your children.
Acts 20:35	• Give, and it shall be given unto you; good measure, pressed down, and shaken together, and running over, shall men give into your bosom.....
3 John 1:2	• For I know the thought that I think toward you, saith the LORD, thoughts of peace, and not of evil, to give you an expected end.
Deuteronomy 8:18	• Beloved, I wish above all things that thou mayest prosper and be in health, even as thy soul prospereth.
Jeremiah 29:11	• .....It is more blessed to give than to receive.

List additional wealth scriptures:

_____

_____

_____

_____

_____

_____

_____

_____

_____

_____

_____

_____

_____

_____

_____

_____

_____

_____

_____

_____

_____

_____

_____

_____

_____

_____

_____

QUESTIONS

How was the subject matter beneficial to you?

_____

_____

_____

_____

_____

_____

_____

_____

_____

_____

_____

_____

_____

_____

_____

_____

_____

_____

_____

Will you continue to use this information to maintain and sustain your financial success? If so, How?

_____

_____

_____

_____

_____

_____

_____

_____

_____

_____

_____

_____

_____

_____

_____

_____

_____

_____

_____

_____

_____

_____

List the names of people who you know will benefit from this book?

_____

_____

_____

_____

_____

_____

_____

_____

_____

_____

_____

_____

_____

_____

_____

_____

_____

_____

_____

_____

_____

_____

_____

GRATITUDE

Thank you for your support. I pray that you receive and take appropriate action to your road of newness to experiencing life in abundance as you change your mindset and speech toward your finances. You will be completely financially free by walking in total abundance of wealth. We decree a wealthy mindset and wealthy speech... It is the new YOU!

<u>NOTES</u>

_____

_____

_____

_____

_____

_____

_____

_____

_____

_____

_____

_____

_____

_____

_____

_____

_____

_____

_____

_____

<u>NOTES</u>

_____

_____

_____

_____

_____

_____

_____

_____

_____

_____

_____

_____

_____

_____

_____

_____

_____

_____

_____

_____

_____

_____

TESTIMONIALS

"I met with Olivers Financial Planning in 2015, wanting to better manage my finances and create a savings plan. Mrs. Oliver's service was absolutely impeccable! Following her expert advice, I could re-organize my income to almost triple my saving potential. She is extremely insightful and keen to the financial industry. Most of all, she cares about her clients and puts her heart into making them successful. I readily recommend this company to anyone looking to have financial freedom!"

    — Jaquetta Ross

"A few years ago, I received assistance from Stacey because I needed a practical perspective about where I was financial. My finances had changed dramatically and I was used to a certain lifestyle. Stacey helped me see everything on paper and weed out what I could get rid of and how to shift money around to keep living. Her knowledge, background and expertise were what I needed to help me make things make sense and work! If you need practical advice

and assistance making money work; she's
the one you need to see. Thanks Stacey!"
— *Juanita Jones*

ABOUT THE AUTHOR

Stacey Oliver firmly believes to be financially successful is greatly determined by individuals' ability to take ownership of their financial livelihood. Unfortunately for many, financial literacy education is scarce, if not completely unavailable.

Her mission is to "create, enlighten, and empower committed effective stewards of finances; focusing intensely on increasing individuals' knowledge of financial freedom within the community of various demographics while removing the vicious cycle and hold of debt".

With over seventeen years of experience as a public Financial Literacy speaker, certified banker, and serving on various boards and committees for financial wellness in the upstate of South Carolina, Stacey Oliver has established herself as an expert in the field. She helps individuals and families unlock doors of financial barriers with NO DOUBT.

Stacey uses her "gift of gab" to coach and empower audiences with the "Master Key" of knowledge to obtaining and sustaining financial success.

Stacey Oliver is also the founder of Financial Kick Start JBJO, Inc., Non-Profit Organization. Noted by many as the *"Financial Locksmith"*, she reserves a special space at Financial Kick Start JBJO for sowing into the lives of individuals.

When you find her not ministering through her business, organization, and daily routine, Stacey is enjoying life with her family and friends.

For book presentations or more information on how you can take advantage of our services, contact:

STACEY M. OLIVER,
CEO/Founder

®™

Olivers Financial Planning Services, LLC
(aka OFPS, LLC)
www.ofpsagency.com

Instagram/@oliversfps

Facebook/@OliversFPS

Twitter/@Ofpsllc